ARE YOU
READY
TO
COMPETE?

Also by John Gaglione:

The Powerlifting Handbook

Powerlifting For The People

ARE YOU READY TO COMPETE

BY
JOHN GAGLIONE

Copyright 2019 © Gaglione Strength All rights reserved.
ISBN-13: 978-1-073-036813

Please visit www.gaglionestrength.com for more information regarding our programs.

Instagram: @gaglionestrength
Email Address: john@gaglionestrength.com

Table of Contents

Introduction

WHO AM I? HOW DID I get involved in powerlifting competitions, coaching, and competing for the past dozen years?

So you are thinking about getting involved in powerlifting? I made that choice right as my high school years ended and I haven't looked back! It has been one of the best decisions I have made for myself... but is it right for you?

For that don't know me people call me Coach Gaglione! I've been involved with powerlifting for over a decade and have been competing for the past 12 years (going on 13 as I finish writing this book)!

I got my start at just 18 years old, and over the years, I've seen a lot of trends come and go, and I've watched it really evolve. When I first started, there might be about 20-30 competitors at a local event and maybe up to 40 for the bigger events.

Now, we'll go to competitions that have 40 to 60

and even some with 120 lifters just in the course of one weekend. And sometimes, the events would have to be split up into multiple sessions just to accommodate all the competitors.

The sport is clearly growing in interest and popularity. With that, though, I've noticed that a lot of the newer lifters get lost in the shuffle and not no where to start and may not be fully prepared. So out of the kindness of my heart, I'll find myself and our team helping some of the newer lifters in the warm up room just to help them get their bearings at many of the local contests.

I realize that as a new competitor, entering an event with over 100 people can be daunting, filled with lots of questions and concerns. There's a lot of unknown, which for most people is a scary thing. My goal, since I came onto the scene before this surge, is to help the newer competitors adjust properly and have a great first experience with powerlifting.

With the popularity of CrossFit, people started to grow really interested in lifting and not be afraid of the barbell anymore, which has contributed to the interest overall, especially for women. When I first started, there were barely any women in even in the crowd. Now, we might have anywhere between 20-40 women competing at a local contest and some even have a whole day devoted to just female lifters!

The sport is clearly also showing greater diverse interest, but not just for sex – we're getting a huge influx of younger lifters, like junior and teenage lifters. There's a general growing interest in the importance of getting strong, and this is what we're going to discuss in this book.

* * *

Our first book, Powerlifting for the People, discusses how adding strength can be a benefit for your body, whether you're an athlete, a senior, a man or a woman, or if you're looking to get lean or add muscle or eventually compete. There are so many benefits to working on your strength, and powerlifting is the perfect vehicle for that. The hurdle is simply now knowing where to start. Training for competition and general health are two different animals entirely and you have to plan accordingly.

ARE YOU READY TO COMPETE?

So many people know that strength training is important and that it's something that want to be involved in, but discovering that first step is often the trickiest. From signing up to a competition, to training for it, to adjusting the diet, there are so many facets that many beginners are unsure of.

Some new lifters may have the means to hire a personal coach, but for those that don't, I wanted to create this resource to help those interested in the sport. I want to ensure that their first experience is positive since the first impression is the one that sets the tone and matters the most.

My hope is that this encouragement and guidance will help grow the sport and allow these new competitors to have a long and fruitful powerlifting journey, whether it's just for fun or as a high-level competitor. My hope is that they have a great first experience and that these steps and tricks in this book helps lifters feel more comfortable, prepared, and confident in the great world of powerlifting.

Ultimately, powerlifting is a mindset, a mental

sport as much as it is a physical one. It's about preparation: the more prepared you are, the more at ease you'll feel. You might feel anxious, but your nerves will lessen, you'll feel that excitement, and you won't be second-guessing yourself.

My old wrestling coach used to ask us, "Would you be afraid to fight a first grader?" Chuckling, we looked at each other and shook our heads. Of course, we knew what the outcome would be – we'd win. That confidence is transferable to your first competition: if you're prepared and if you have a clear idea of what the outcome should be, your chance of success is going to be much higher. If you bring that mindset with you, it'll allow for a great transition into the sport.

When the outcome is clear you will feel more excitement versus anxiety when approaching a powerlifting competition or any important event in your life in general. The better your preparation the more confidence you will have when approaching the platform. Now don't get me wrong even after a dozen years of competing I still get those "butterflies" before my opening lift but I now have a better handle on how to control my emotions and I am a much better lifter on the platform as a result.

About Me and Our Mission

I have mentioned before been involved in coaching athletes and powerlifting for the past 12 years. This has provided me some unique experiences versus just any average joe who lifts weights.

At my gym in Long Island, New York, we've helped over 60 lifters reach national ranks in the sport. One of these athletes, Larry Williams, broke two all-time world records and two different weight classes – one of which, he broke twice. He's currently the world record holder in 242 and 275 weight classes in new sleeves. In addition to Larry, we've had five other athletes reach the top 20 in the world in their weight class and division.

We're not just focused on breaking records, though. We really want to focus on helping those that are just starting out in the sport. The majority of the lifters we coach are novices and early intermediate level lifters just starting out. That being said the fact our system and guidance has produced some of the best lifters in the country and even in the world does say a lot. Our method and training philosophy can work for all levels.

At our gym we want to give them a place where they feel comfortable and confident. We've developed a Powerlifting for the People podcast, which at the start specifically focused on interviewing our women powerlifters; we tell their story of how they got involved in the sport, what they've learned from their mistakes, and advice for other women interested in becoming involved with powerlifting. Since starting our podcast we have also interviewed a wide variety of lifters ranging from world class to those just starting out as well as giving tips on programming, nutrition, and general training knowledge. If you are newer lifters looking to subscribe to that program on Itunes (Powerlifting for the People) and Youtube (GaglioneStrength) to learn from other people's past experience can be an invaluable tool on your journey to completing your first competition.

We also recommending investing in the development of references for those interested in powerlifting. Our first book, Powerlifting for the People, outlines the importance of strength no matter your goals. Our second, The Powerlifting Handbook: Practical Principles for Crushing PRs, is more a principles and programming guide, a collection of our methodologies and philosophies in training. It's a culmination of why we do what we do from a scientific standpoint, yet we also formatted it so that it's still easily digestible. I also do my best to spread our general awareness to the rest of the world – I have been a columnist for Elite FTS and have written for Men's Health and T-Nation. I've spoken at colleges all over the country to talk about the sport and its mindset.

At the end of the day, our motto is to educate, motivate, and dominate. We want to make sure that we provide quality education people are inspired and motivated to train. We want them to dominate in all areas of their life and be successful and reach their goals.

Chapter 1: Getting Started

IT CAN BE DIFFICULT KNOWING where to start if you're interested in the competing aspect of powerlifting. While I do stand that working with a coach is the best since it takes a lot of the guesswork out of the process, I want this guide to be for everyone, coach or no coach.

I encourage interested competitors to first discuss the goal at hand with loved ones to not only hear yourself express your goals, but it's always helpful to discuss them with others that have your best interest at heart. Mapping out your goals on paper is just as beneficial, as there's a certain level of accountability that takes place once those things are committed in writing. The more specific you are in those goals, the better; if your experience level is brand new, this may be difficult to communicate, but the more measurable your goals are, the easier it is to map out an action plan.

You also want these goals to be attainable. If you've never lifted before, you may not be starting out with a 1,000-lb squat. A good starting point instead is squatting roughly one and a half times your body weight, depending on your starting athletic ability. This is challenging yet doable for the next couple of months as you begin your training.

Along with these goals, you'll want to establish a timeline. I'll use myself as an example: I had a competition set for April 14th back in 2018. In preparation of that day, I had the goal of a hit squat of 800 bench 500 and a 675 deadlift in the 242 class. With that end-goal in mind, I was able to formulate how I'd reach that goal from my initial abilities. I ended up squatting 770, benching 490 and deadlifting 640. So even though I didn't reach my goal it provided a target for me to strive towards and I got pretty darn close!

242 Meet

ARE YOU READY TO COMPETE?

It is important to make your goals specific and measurable but don't beat yourself up if you fall a little short your first time working toward them. The old story of the turtle versus the hair applies here. Take your time and be consistent for the long haul. In the end a steady pace wins the race!

In addition to drafting your goals and your timeline, it's also just as important to understand the reasons WHY you want to accomplish these goals, why it's important for me to compete. For me, as a coach, it's important that I lead by example, that I'm leading the front. I want to show people that they can be strong. I want to show people that these methods can work no matter how busy you are. I want to show people that they can be successful and still have a balanced life, maintain a successful business, and still get stronger and do well at any level.

Since the beginning, it's always been really important to me that I'm walking the walk. It carries more power than just spewing inspirational messages. If I fall short of my goals, I have to recognize that it's not the end of the world, yet at the same time, it's helping me refine my target. Once you've narrowed your target and established exactly what you want to achieve, you have to then figure out the why.

The more you define your why, the easier it is to figure out the how. If you're a parent, you want to be strong for your kids. If you're a son or a daughter, and you want to build strength for athletics, you want to make your parents proud. Perhaps you're shy and want to gain self-confidence. It's often that a strong, physical body will lead to a stronger mental and emotional mind.

To achieve all these things, you need to dig deep and figure out why you actually want to do this. I won't lie to you – it's hard and even uncomfortable at times. There will be times when you may hit a plateau, and you may have good workouts and bad workouts. You've got to learn how to roll with the punches. That is why you need to fall in love with the process. Not every day is going to be sunshine and rainbows. This is why knowing your "why" behind working toward your goal is SO important. Once you have that down, you can really connect to your whys. From there, it will be a lot easier to follow through with your goals and work towards a competition. If you have a superficial reason for competing or getting stronger you won't stick to it in the long haul when things actually get hard.

This competition, of course, will completely depend on your level as well as how far away it is in time – it could be three months to a year out. For most beginners, 12 to 16 weeks is plenty of time to prepare for a competition, as long as you don't have a lot of injuries and have decent athletic ability and mobility. If you do not, for any reason, or if you're brand new to training, my recommendation is that you start with push pull where you only perform two out of three competition lifts or a single lift meet.

At Gaglione Strength we offer deadlift only meets as well as a charity bench press competition to help encourage new lifters to compete with a low barrier of entry. This allows the lifter to "get their feet wet" and they won't need as much training time as prepping for a full meet with all three competition lifts.

Competition Bench Press

Basically, the sport of powerlifting is three lifts, the squat, the bench press, and the dead lift. In one federation called United States Strength Lifting they swap the bench press for the standing overhead press.

In my opinion, that is a good order of the lifts and this is why I think it is performed in this manner. The squat has probably the most mobility and athletic requirements to it, which I believe is why it's placed first. The bench press is a little bit more of an upper body test, whereas a squat is a little bit more of a lower body test of strength. The deadlift is a full-body lift, but It's mostly a test of your back strength as well.

Most people can do a dead lift so long as you can tie your shoes and reach your ankles; you may not necessarily be able to touch your toes, but you should be able to just bend over as though you're picking something up off the ground. Most people, even those in their later years, can be able to dead lift. Practicing this is a great place to start as a beginner, and from there, I'd recommend moving on to a push pull, which would be a bench and a deadlift and eventually a three lift meet.

For information on Finding Powerlifting events in your area you can check out **http://www.powerliftingwatch.com** and click the events tab and search for you meet in your home or surrounding states.

There are some special cases like lifter with spinal cord injuries, amputees or other disabilities that prevent them from doing any form of lower body lifts and squatting or deadlifting is not possible. For athlete in special cases like this athletes could participate in bench only meet where the use of their lower body is not required in order to compete. In special cases they could also train and compete in a Para Powerlifting competition. These are more rare and hard to find but they use a special bench in which athletes are able to strap their legs onto a special bench for competition taking the lower body completely out of the equation.

You can check out
https://www.disabledpowerlifting.com
for more information about Para Powerlifting Competitions and if you qualify to compete in them.

As you become more comfortable, you can participate in a full competition, though it doesn't have to be full right away. As long as you are able to do the movements with an empty barbell, which is 45 pounds or about 20 kilograms, you should be physically ready to compete. Of course, most people don't want to lift just the empty barbell, but it's a great place to start.

In some federations the squat bar might be as heavy at 55-65 lbs and a special bench bar might be 50 lbs. So I would say once you can squat over

65 lbs bench over 45 lbs and deadlift over 95 lbs you are "strong enough" to compete.

For people starting out you can use broom sticks, hollow bars or a women's weightlifting bar which typically weights about 33 lbs to get started before progressing into the full size barbell.

Once you're ready to do the movements with competition technique, you can start to figure out how to prepare for your competition. From there, I'd recommend finding a coach so you can learn how to lift properly according to competition standard. A good resource for powerlifting is powerliftingwatch.com. On this site, there's a section that includes all the meets, so you can check out all the competitions in your state. You can also find a powerlifting-friendly gym so you can make sure you have the proper training equipment.

If you're looking for a coach it is best to find one with a lot of experience both competing and coaching. Usually someone with over 10 years of experience is a very safe bet. Don't just hire someone because they have a strong body or a big total. Just because someone is a good lifter doesn't mean they are a good coach. Look at people they have worked with and see how they have progressed overtime.

For powerlifting gyms you can simply do some research on the gyms in your area or check out their social media on different platforms like Instagram, Facebook and Youtube to see if the gym is a good fit .

Another great preparation recommendation I have is to attend a meet as a spectator before the meet you plan on competing in. This is a great chance for you to network—meet coaches, other athletes, or other like-minded powerlifters. This is your chance to connect with them and maybe even establish a buddy system for training. Local clinics and seminars are also becoming more common.

Try to find a clinic where you can get some hands on coaching so you can learn the lifts properly before embarking on a full training program without having the proper technique in place.

Next, it's critical that you learn the movements properly. You can learn these moves from a coach, other lifters, or even sources online; try to surround yourself with lifters that are a little bit more knowledgeable so that you can practice the movements and learn from them. Of course, there are plenty of video tutorials online, but use your best judgment should you choose to check these out.

To really get the most value out of your coach, I obviously recommend finding someone that's experienced. As I mentioned before I generally use a 10-year level of experience as a rule of thumb – this tells me that they know what they're doing. It'll also help if you talk to others that this coach may have worked with before to get their feedback.

Once you feel you have your movements down to good competition standards, pick out a meet about 12 to 16 weeks away. If you're on the beginner side, perhaps find one even later than that. From there, it's time to start your training. In the beginning, simply add a little bit of weight every workout to the bar. Depending on your size and starting strength, it could be 5 to 10 pounds. As you get closer to your meet date, do less repetitions and heavier weight, like a heavy set of two or three. All you need to do is get a feel of where you are and where you should start, and then you can test out your numbers at the meet.

Every person's training program will be different than the next, and you'll learn to adapt this as you grow. To provide a very simple and broad example of building a program for yourself, consider a six-week development. The first week, you'll work up to a heavy set of eight, then five weeks out, you'll switch to a heavy set of six, and then the following week a heavy set of four, and then shuffle, switch to a double single, then rest the week of. Again, this is very broad and generic, but it should still provide a clear structure of how you should conduct your program for your first program.

Here is an example of a basic linear progression to peak you for a 1RM to get you ready for a contest. Let's say in week one the athlete is able to do one set of the deadlift with 200 lbs for 5 repetitions. Each week they add a little weight while keeping good form. As they increase the weight the reps will need to drop over time.

Wk 1 200x5 -- *Wk 2* 205x5 -- *Wk 3* 210 x5

Wk 4 215x5 -- *Wk 5* 220x5 -- *Wk 6* 225x4

Wk 7 230x3 -- *Wk 8* 235x3 -- *Wk 9* 240x3

Wk 10 245x2 -- *Wk 10* 250x1 -- *Wk 11* 255x1

Wk 12 225x1 -- Rest until meet

In this fictional scenario the novice lifter is able to end their linear progression at 255 for a new one rep maximum. The week of the meet they drop the weight a rest a bit before the contest. The lifter might open with 235 at their contest and then go up to 245 or 250 on a 2nd attempt and then hit 255-265 for a new personal record on their 3rd attempt. For the first competition the program doesn't need to be extravagant. Over time add more weight and drop the reps as the meet or testing day gets closer BUT always be mindful of form.

To recap, start by first defining your goal. Why do you want the goal? Next, look into coaching for your lifts until you get comfortable and more confident. After that, you should pick out your competition and decide how you'll prepare for the meet. There are tons of programs out there and many different methods.

Obviously, receiving some sort of programming from a coach for your technique would be ideal, but there are many different programs that can be offered. We offer programs that help our lifters reach their desired potential; you just have to find the right one for you.

Our Available Programs

A lot of people have specific interest in the programs that I offer in our gym. On our site gaglionestrength.com, there's a tab for distance coaching for any kind of competition you're participating in. You can also feel free to message me directly at *gaglionestrength@gmail.com*. I make an effort to answer every single message I get!

I also have a link that will then ask for some contact information from you and put you on a list to set up a free consultation. We also have our world record holder programs that Larry Williams and many other of our athletes have used to break national and world records—essentially, there's a program on there for any skill level. If you were to do all of the programs together, it would give you a 20-week cycle.

For information about getting coaching and programming use this link

https://power.gaglionestrength.com

If you're a beginner, this 20-week cycle is a bit on the long site but also a really great place to start. Basically you do eight weeks of hypertrophy training, which is essentially designed to building the foundation and your core muscle capacity. From there, you'll complete about six weeks of strength training, which is a moderate rep training to really build maximal strength. After that we'll enter a peaking phase and be a bit more focused on the narrow drive and using lower repetitions to realize the strength you build up in subsequent phases . During the final phase we can really stack on the heavyweights and stimulate the nervous system.

For a bit more background on hypertrophy

training, this could be anywhere from six to eight to 10 to even 12 weeks. This sets the foundation for heavy lifting to come later on. There is an old saying "you can't flex bone" so this phase is designed to build muscle with higher rep ranges and using exercise that typically have a longer range of motion and higher time under tension to stimulate muscle fibers and ultimately growth. A bigger muscle often times yields a stronger muscle.

Strength training should be about five or six reps – or less. Lower rep training will allow you to use more weight. Heavy weights are the best way to get strong. This is why a lot of powerlifters and strength training programs focus on reps of 5. 5 rep sets are a good in between rep range that can help build muscle and strength at the same time. After a good amount of time in the medium rep range it's then best to focus on singles, doubles, and triples since those rep ranges are going to have the highest carry over to hitting a new one rep max at the contest.

During a peaking cycle overloading exercise that allow you to handle more than your current one rep max as well as special exercises to make sure you're getting your technique right for the contest as also encouraged. The goal of a peaking cycle is to make sure you are in your top form come game day. Doing this requires a careful combination of stimulating the nervous system while dropping fatigue which is why when training loads and intensity is up the volume and amount of sets and reps you do must go down. This is the best way to break up the training, but of course, if you need more direction or resources, just check out the distance coaching tab on our site.

During peaking and strength training phases it important that you lower your volumes (amount of sets and reps) because it's going to drop your fatigue and allow your body to rest for the competition so you can perform your best. Depending on your sex, you can either do a week or a couple of days of a deload so you could tapper and realize your best potential on the platform. No matter how intricate your program is this is a great way to approach the contest. For more information on our programming methods you should check out the Powerlifting Handbook on Amazon as well.

If you're in the Long Island or New York area, we do also host events throughout the year. In February, we have our deadlift contest, and in June, we have a full meet. In December, we have an event just four our youth and novice lifters, which is a great starting point if you're a beginner. We have an up-to-date events tab on our site if you want more information.

For information on coaching, programs and future events check out *gaglionestrength.com*

Chapter 2: Next Steps for Competition

So say you've laid out your goals and received some fundamental training. You've picked out your meet and now you're ready to start your program. Now what? What's the process look like?

Every federation is different. Some may have some sort of user technology to collect information, and others might have some kind of federation membership for insurance and liability reasons. The meet will be sanctioned, which basically just means that the contest is going to be official, so any results will be essentially "on the books." You numbers will go into a rankings system on Open Powerlifting as well as Powerlifting Watch. Open powerlifting is a large database where you can see how you rank across your weight class, division, and age group.

While hitting ranks may not be important to you as you're starting out, you'd be surprised at how appealing it is once you start the competition process. You'll see people climbing and improving their ranks, which may inspire you to do the same. Perhaps you want to be nationally ranked or to qualify for a higher level or national or even a money meet. You'll usually need to have a qualifying total to do so, and in a specific federation or contest, you'll have to hit a certain number and weight press. That's why sanctioning and becoming a member of the federation is important.

The Revolution Powerlifting Syndicate (RPS) doesn't actually require or have a membership fee to join, unlike every other federation. Regardless, you need to become a member of a federation, which can easily be done through the federation's website. Since each federation is different, the rules and equipment that are used will be different.

RPS Meet

The signing up process is fairly simple once your membership is active. A great site to use to check out events near you is powerliftingwatch. com. This resource has filters so you can search by location and date. So if you're looking for a meet that's 12 to 16 weeks out while you're just getting started, you can easily click on the links provided and simply sign up for it, making yourself accountable for the training.

Of course, in today's world, most of us are used to making payments online quickly and easily, but some gyms, like mine, still provide the option to mail in the entry form and check. The entry form will have different categories of lifting. For anyone's first meet, most of the time they'll want to just do the raw category. Again, this changes a bit depending on the federation, but the raw category simply implies that it is minimal equipment, meaning that you can wear wrist wraps and a belt. Some federations also allow knee sleeves for support. Make sure you check the rules of the federation so you can "practice how you play" and train using competition legal equipment and attire.

As you climb through the ranks and improve your skills, there are also different categories. One is called a raw with wraps category, and if you prefer to lift in knee wraps for the squat, that would be a separate category. There are also things like single ply equipment and multi-ply equipment. If you want to get into wearing a bench shirt, a squat suit, or a deadlift suit, that's a different category as well as a different type of lifting.

Raw Squat

Wrapped Squat

Equipped Squat

I would advise for your first meet just go raw. Raw typically means a belt and wrist wraps and most federations (RPS does not) allow knee sleeves for the raw division. Anything on your knees would put you in a raw modern division for the RPS but you would still be grounded in the raw division nationally as long as you indicate your are wearing knee sleeves and not knee wraps to the meet director.

Certain federations may offer only single ply or multi ply for equipped lifting, but again, that's another category. Most beginners will want to start in the raw category. There is also an age group and a weight class. You could be in the teenage group or be in the junior lifter age group, which is age 20-23. If you're over the age of 23, you can also choose to be grouped together with everyone else and participate in the open division. Everyone has different reasons for wanting to be in an age group (or not), so it's important to consider that when signing up for your competitions.

If you're over the age of 40, you also have the option of entering something called a master's division. You'd then be competing against others in this age category. If you're looking for a higher competition, however, I'd recommend competing in the open division. My recommendation is just sign up for the age group in which you belong, and as you get more competitive, you can choose to be more flexible about the age groups you enter. You may find you might be able to break state or federation records in a certain age group so if that is a goal by all means sign up for that category if you meet the requirements!

Master Lifter

ARE YOU READY TO COMPETE?

Teen Lifter

Once your age group is established, you'll need to figure out your weight class. While this is an important factor in your overall competition strategy, I recommend that in the beginning, you don't focus to much on losing a certain amount of weight or gaining a specific level of muscle to fit into any certain weight class. Simply put, just start your first competition at your starting weight, and as your body develops and responds more to the training, your body will tell you what weight class you should be in. To recap DO NOT CUT WEIGHT FOR YOUR FIRST COMPETITION!!!!

As an example, let's say you currently weigh 205 pounds. In most federations, there is a 198-pound weight class, and then there is a 220-pound weight class. Even though you're closer to the 198-pound class, I'd recommend, especially for your first competition, not to worry about losing weight to hit the lower mark. Losing that weight is another factor that could potentially hinder your performance. I would instead worry about the training and feeling good, and certainly do not starve yourself – make sure you're well-fed and that your nutrition is good and well-balanced. So in this case this lifter would sign up for the 220 class for this meet since this lifter weights in excess of 198 lbs.

Whatever weight class you're under (and not over), I would choose to enter that weight class for your first competition. As you get more competitive and versed on the ways of competing, it's safer to explore the possibility of entering the lower weight class if you choose. Some lifters find that this can give them a greater chance for national level qualifications or an American or an all-time world record, but these competitors are highly trained, so be careful when making these decisions. There are ways to effectively and healthily do this, so I recommend discussing this with your coach or a trusted and fellow powerlifter. In my experience if you aren't in contention for a qualifying total or some sort of substantial federation or person record I rarely see the need for someone to cut weight going into a powerlifting competition.

Again, for the time being, I would recommend entering the weight class that you're under and not stress about being a few pounds over or under. Your first competition is there to give you experience, to have a good time, and to get a good feel of the world of competitive powerlifting. You definitely want to limit the amount of variables that can go wrong and avoid any variables that might hinder your performance or overall enjoyment of the experience.

In essence, this is kind of how the sign-up process will work for these events. Some meets may have some sort of Facebook event page, and some meets may add you to some kind of mailing list to provide you with information about the meet and send along any updates or changes along the way. It's pretty simple and not a lot to it.

Here is a helpful chart for the national recognized weight classes in every Federation except the USAPL.

Men's		Women's	
KG	LBs	KG	LBs
0-52	114.64	0-44	97
52.01 –56	123.45	44.01 – 48	105.82
56.01 –60	132.27	48.01 – 52	114.64
60.01 – 67.5	148.81	52.01 – 56	123.45
67.51 –75	165.35	56.01 – 60	132.27
75.01 -82.5	181.88	60.01 – 67.5	148.81
82.51 – 90	198.41	67.51 –75	165.35
90.01 –100	220.46	75.01 – 82.5	181.88
100.01-110	242.5	82.51 – 90	198.42
110.01 –125	275.57	90.01 –100	220.46 (RPS Only)
125.01 –140	308.65	100.01 –110	242.5 (RPS Only)
140.01– unlimited	SHW	100.01 – unlimited	SHW

Chapter 3: Choosing Your Meet & Federations

CHOOSING YOUR FIRST MEET IS both exciting and probably a little bit overwhelming and nerve-wracking. It can be stressful trying to figure out an event that's right for you as a beginner, and as the popularity of the sport continues to grow, it might feel like you have too many options or too many people to compete with.

For your first meet, we recommend meets that are a little bit lower pressure and can provide lifters more options in the beginning as you're starting out. Some federations are a little bit more stringent with the rules, and they may not allow us as much leeway as others. This could be as small as the t-shirt you choose to wear or the singlet you're allowed to wear. Again, as I mentioned earlier, I'm a big advocate for the Revolution Powerlifting Syndicate (RPS).

There are a lot of great benefits that come with working with the Revolution Powerlifting

Syndicate. First of all, it's a very well-run and organized meet, which is incredibly important as the number of participants in this sport continues to grow every year. The RPS also provides a lot of options for lifters. They could potentially do the raw category, or they could do a raw with wraps category. They could choose to participate in the single ply category, or they could do the multi ply category. Many federation don't have as many options that cater to as many lifters. No matter the skill level you are as a lifter, you can compete in the RPS meet. Other federations may not have all of these categories available, but it's great that the RPS does. As a coach myself, I appreciate this since I have lifters of all shapes and sizes and ability levels.

Another benefit of the RPS is that if you prefer to wear something on your knee while you compete, you can do a raw modern, which means that if you want to wear knee sleeves or knee wraps, you can do so in the raw modern category. If you want to instead just wear a belt and wrist wraps and nothing on your knees, you can do so in the raw classic category.

ARE YOU READY TO COMPETE?

The RPS allows for more flexibility for certain moves as well. If you prefer to walk out of your squat or use the mono lift (the device where you stand up out of the hooks and the cradle moves while the hooks move so that you don't have to walk out of the weight), this federation tends to be much more understanding of personal preference, something that I appreciate as well.

So if you prefer to walk up your squats like you would do out of a normal power rack, you can do so. If you prefer to use the mono-lifts it could be very useful if you are a knee wrap lifter or an equipped lifter in the single or multi ply division.

The mono lift also has safety straps, which helps protect the lifter if he or she loses control of the bar, avoiding a catastrophic injury due to the spotters not getting to the bar in time. You don't get this safety feature when competing in a meet that uses squat stands which leads us into our next point.

Mono Lift

Other federations and other meets use squat stands instead of mono lifts. The benefit to a squat stand is that it's easier to set up for a meet director, but in my opinion, it's simply not as safe as a mono lift because there is no safety apparatus that can catch the bar if the spotter misses it. Potentially there could be more chance of injury for a meet from stands than a mono lift. For a meet that uses a stand, of course you'd have to walk the weight out. There is no option to use a mono lift – there is no option to simply stand up with the weight.

This is something to consider when choosing a meet as safety is a factor no matter how prepared you are. Things can happen. Spotters are human and make mistakes and sometimes injuries can happen with a blink of an eye. I like knowing our lifters are safe just in case something does happen on game day. Accidents can happen even with careful preparation and smart training. Safety should always be a consideration when picking a meet.

Larry Failing at US Open (1)

Larry Failing at US Open (2)

The bench press also has certain requirements through the RPS federation. It allows you to bench press with your heels down, either flat on the floor or up so you can bench on the balls of your feet. That's a personal preference. Some people are more comfortable benching on the balls of their feet, while others are more comfortable with benching with their flat feet. The RPS will also allow you to have your own hand-off person.

The RPS federation allows you to get lift-off from a partner during a bench press. In other federations, you have to use designated spotters, and those spotters may not be able to put the bar exactly where you want it. They also may be unfamiliar with communicating with you and putting the bar where you actually need it. This can be hugely problematic and throw you off your set-up. I like the RPS because you can use your own hand-off person and allow for more repeated hand-offs to allow your lifter to sit up properly on the bench press.

In federations that don't allow for your own hand off person some lifters will even elect to take the bar out themselves so they have more consistency at a meet. In my opinion this create a disadvantage and can waste important energy you would otherwise use toward actually bench pressing the weight.

Bench Press Hand-off

Some meet directors will argue having a designated spotter is important for safety but in my opinion it's mainly just to keep the platform more organized and prevent people who don't belong on the platform from getting on their in the first place. I can see both sides of the coin but from a lifter perspective it is nice to have someone you personally know hand you off or center you under the bar for the squat. It creates a better experience for the lifter in my opinion.

I also like the RPS because of the deadlift allowances. For this event, you can actually compete barefoot or actually not have to wear shoes. Some people prefer this style for this event and compete shoeless or sockless. This allows them to get a little bit lower to the ground, it allows them to sit back a little bit more, and it cuts down on the range and motion a little bit for the deadlift. Most other federations require you to wear some sort of shoe, and sometimes, especially when a lifter is starting out, they may not have a lot of extra funds to buy the special shoes for both the squat and deadlift events.

In all other federation you are required to have

some sort of foot wear in the deadlift and usually high socks to prevent the lifter from being in direct contact with the bar and their skin. It's nice that if someone wants to just deadlift barefoot, they could, or if they wanted deadlift in their socks, they could do that as well.

Deadlift picure showing socks

Of course, these are all just some of the differences from RPS and the rest of the federations, but they're all reasons I prefer them. The RPS will also use special barbells, which to me, help aid the performance of the lift. The squat bar is a little bit thicker, which will allow for less oscillation of the weight plates, so it will be a more stable squat for the lifter. The bench bar is a little bit longer, so it allows for easier and more safe spotting on the bench press.

The RPS also has the best safety not only for the squat but the bench as well. In the bench press they use "face savers." In my opinion, it's much safer to bench press with face savers on. Basically, it's job is to catch the bar if the spotters miss it for some reason just like the safety straps due for the squat.

For the deadlift, they use a special deadlift bar, which allows for a little bit more flex and a little bit more width. Typically, if you know how to use the bar properly, and if you pull the slack out, it's a little bit easier on the lower back and allows for a little bit of a more comfortable starting position for the deadlift, as opposed to using a stiff bar which doesn't have as much flex or as much whip.

In any event you DO NOT need to do an RPS meet for your first contest but it's something I would highly recommend. There are plenty of other options you can try if those meets aren't in your area. At the end of the day the most important thing is the meet director and the people running the meet itself. The people running the show dictate how the rules are interpreted and deliver the experience directly to the competitors.

While that's one extreme, another would be the USAPL (USA Powerlifting), the biggest drug-tested federation, and we have had a lot of lifters compete in this realm. It's probably the most competitive federation. A lot of the top lifters and more serious lifters compete in the USAPL. In my opinion, it's probably best to avoid the USAPL for your first competition; they don't necessarily care if it's your first time. Instead, they expect you to know the rules whether you're new or not.

Coaching at USAPL Meet

They will hold you to a very high standard no matter what level you're at. This is a good thing to keep competitions and the standard of lifting consistent but there are downsides to this for brand new lifters too. This is just something to keep in mind that this may not be the best choice for your first competition.

If you're very competitive, extremely strong for your age and weight class, and have been at the sport for years, then I'd say the idea to compete in the USAPL could make sense. Certainly, if you're trying to get on a world team and represent your country and are one of the best athletes in the country or maybe perhaps you're one of the strongest lifters in the world, then the USAPL would be a good fit.

The USAPL federation has a lot of different rules. You must walk out your squats at a stand. You must keep your head down, and your head needs to stay in contact with the bench. Your feet need to stay flat on the ground, and your heels must be down on the bench press. The deadlift, the squat, and the bench press all use the same bar, and it's a little bit of a stiffer bar, which makes the deadlift a little bit more challenging since it will be more difficult to pull off the floor. This makes running a meet more efficient but it makes the lifts a bit more challenging to perform. The bars they use for the USAPL aren't very stable and can whip a lot when squatting heavy and for deadlifts the bar doesn't flex at all which makes the lift harder from the floor and can cause more stress to the lower back compared to the thinner whippier deadlift bar used in federations like the RPS, USPA and UPA.

The rules also apply to the equipment with the USAPL, and there are some pieces of equipment that aren't even allowed. There are a many belts, singlets, and logos that are not allowed. For example we have team single with our gym logo and those would not be permitted at a USAPL competition. It is unfortunate that a lifter could not represent the gym and club they train with at a local USAPL meet. There is a strict equipment check and even things like the underwear your use could be prohibited in competition. Overall, there are many more restrictions and a lot more red tape when you go into the USAPL.

These restrictions could make for a challenging experience for someone who is just starting out, especially when they don't have the money to spend on special equipment that is required. RPS has a lot more leeway when it comes to the types of knee wraps, sleeves, wrist wraps, and belts you can use. That being said when it comes to high level competition I think these standards are not just justified they are warranted to keep a level playing field. That being said I don't think it makes sense for a lifter to stress over what singlet they bought or what underwear they typically wear when looking to compete for the first time.

Again, if you're a seasoned veteran, the USAPL could be a great option. For high level competitors the USAPL has the highest competition and is great for people looking to compete among the best of the country. For raw with wraps competitions the equivalent would be USPA for best competition in that division. If you are serious about being one of the best and top drug-free lifters in the country, the USAPL is a great option. For a first competition, I strongly advise against it. At the end of the day this just my opinion based on experience of coaching athletes in all federations at all levels of competition for the past dozen years and I hope it helps you when deciding what to do for your first meet.

The USAPL and the RPS federations are two of the more extreme examples. Other federations have different verbal commands for each lift. In most, there are usually some squat commands to initiate the start of the moment for the squat, and then all federations have a rack command to initiate the end of a squat. In the bench press within most federations, there are also some start commands to initiate the event, commands for after a pause in the bench press, and then commands for the completion. So most federation the commands for squat would be START or SQUAT and then RACK at the finish. For bench would be START or BENCH then PRESS after the pause and then RACK.

In the UPA and the SPF there is no start command for the squat or bench press for example. In Para Powerlifting there is no PRESS command and you must pause the bench on your own and hope the judge likes your pause length. In the United States Strength Lifting Federation there are no verbal commands but you must adhere to similar rules. In all federations in the deadlift event (except in a strength lifting meet), there is a down command once you complete the lift.

There are some differences in how these are done across all federations but there is a lot of overlap in general. It's critical to know what these rules are depending on the federation that you compete in, as there might be more stringent rules in one compared to others. There might be stricter restrictions on equipment and what's allowed during the actual competition. There are all things to keep in mind when choosing a federation and a meet as well as during your training and preparation. If you're geographically located in the Northeast area, I would definitely recommend the RPS for finding meets in your area.

For RPS meet use this link
https://www.revolutionpowerlifting.com

If your preference for competition is for a stricter meet and higher level competitors right out of the gate, of course check out your options at usapowerlifting.com. If you prefer a competition that's a bit down the middle, another option for you is UPA This is also great if you prefer using a mono lift. In a few select states you can also find the WRPF and SPF meets as well.

The USPA (United States Powerlifting Association)– this federation is not as stringent as USAPL. The USPA will use stands to squat out of but will use special barbells for the squat and the deadlift. All of these have meets and calendars that you can reference and sign up for competitions through. This level of meet typically has the highest level of competition for raw with wraps competitors as well as athletes who prefer not to go under drug testing protocols.

Coaching at US Open

The XPC has the highest level of competition for multiply and raw with wraps lifters who specifically like using the monolift. A qualifying total is required to lift at an XPC meet. For single ply and raw lifter the highest level of competition you can achieve in the drug tested division would be USAPL nationals.

ARE YOU READY TO COMPETE?

XPC finals and USAPL Nationals Coaching

Chapter 4: Check-in Process and Establishing Openings

DEPENDING ON THE FEDERATION YOU choose, there will be different things you'll encounter during the check-in process. Many federations have a check-in process for the equipment, so keep that in mind prior to the event—this can be time-consuming, so prepare for that. Additionally, if you don't check-in your equipment the day of the meet and you happen to be wearing something that isn't permitted, the meet director or one of the judges may or may not let you know ahead of time before you get onto the platform.

It's also a great idea to sift through the federation's rule book prior to your competition to ensure you understand what's allowed and what's not. For some brief overview and generalizations, I'll give you some quick insight into what most federations expect. As I mentioned earlier, most have some sort of equipment check-in process. I would make sure prior to the event that you have all of your equipment ready and with you for the competition. While this isn't necessarily the case for all federations, national competitions most often ban underwear that has legs—think boxers or Under Armor biker shorts.

To be safe we recommend to not wear an underwear that has "legs". The main reason federation have implemented this rule is that people have tried to wear a multi ply or a single ply squat brief underneath the singlet and pass it being as raw. This would give the lifter an unfair advantage using supportive equipment in the raw category.

Squat Briefs

The majority of federations also require that you wear long songs for the deadlift, which will protect your shins. Sometimes the bar is dragging against your legs, and these socks will act as a barrier to your skin. You might notice that bleeding can sometimes happen here. Additionally, the socks will also prevent any blood getting on the barbell, which also helps for obvious sanitary and health reasons.

Another clothing requirement is a one-piece lifting suit. This could either be a singlet specifically designed for powerlifting, or it could be a basic wrestling singlet. You can get a ton of options on Amazon, as long as you're doing research on what's appropriate and acceptable. The reason for the singlet requirement is so the judges can see your hip crease throughout the cycle of your lift. Most powerlifting equipment companies such as Inzer, Metal gear, SBD, Titan and a host of other companies other competition legal singlet's that would pass in any federation.

Baggy clothes prohibit this clear view and how your body is performing during the lift. For the squat in the bench in the USAPL, women are also required to wear a shirt, but typically for the squat in the bench, for safety purposes, the shirt is a form of protection so that the bar is not sliding or you are not sliding on the bench.

For the squat and the bench, it'll help you move a bit easier and help ground you a little bit more on the bench press. I believe by the time of this writing the USAPL lifters may also need to wear a shirt in the deadlift as well but most federations do not require a shirt for the deadlift. Check the federation rule book to be sure.

Our Singlet

Typically, you are required to wear some sort of shirt that cannot cover the elbow. The reason for this is because this is a body part that is judged for the bench press and for other lifts. When it comes to equipment, if you're participating in the raw category, or if there's a category in which you'd like to wear wrist wraps, get some compression for the wrist. Elbow sleeves are typically allowed for the squat because they're not a weight-bearing joint.

If you have elbow issues, you can feel free to wear elbow sleeves for the squat to alleviate pain or risk to injury.

Elbow sleeves, however, are not allowed for the bench press. Since this event involves this weight-bearing joint, these sleeves will aid the exercise involved in the lift. If you are in a raw with wraps or a modern division and need to wear knee sleeves, make sure you bring your knee sleeves and wraps prior to your competition check-in.

Lifter wearing elbow sleeves

While a lot of this equipment is not required, you may find you need, like wrist wraps. Usually the singlet and socks and shoes are typical requirements for most federations (with the exception of the RPS, which allows you to be barefoot). Belts, wrist wraps, and knee sleeves are of course all optional, but they can also prove to be great for support. Your belt is usually going to be some sort of leather, so also make sure that the dimensions are fitting within the rules. Often,

Velcro belts are not allowed, or if the belt is too wide and does not fit in within the dimension requirements, it will be allowed. Again, it's wise to look into this before your competition to avoid any last-minute surprises. Most people will use a 10mm or 13mm belt.

When we talk about footwear, there's an old saying: "You don't want to have $100 squat shoes and a 10 cent squat." Basically, you don't necessarily need fancy shoes for your first meet. You can easily get yourself a pair of Chuck Taylor's for $20, and these will probably suit you just fine, but as you improve in the ranks and in your personal strength, it's a good idea to invest in some decent footwear for the competition. You'll find out your preferences as you advance and become more skilled, but there are heeled and flat shoes available – ask around for what others recommend to get a feel of where you think you should start when it comes to your footwear.

Lifter wearing squat shoes

In a nutshell it is best to make sure you equipment is legal ahead of time so bring all of your competition equipment to the equipment check and refer to the federation rule book ahead of time to double check.

Once you're at the stage in which you're checking in, keep in mind your membership status. Every federation has some sort of membership requirement except for RPS. I recommend getting into the habit of bringing the receipt of your membership with you or even your membership card. This will of course prove that you are a member of the federation, which will make the check-in process easier, as they'll have your information handy at the weigh-in. From there, you'll weigh in, and the ideal situation is you'll be under the weight class that you signed up for.

To avoid any weight surprises the day of the event, I simply recommend that you just don't go crazy the night before with the food. Depending on how close you are to your weight class I also wouldn't drink too much liquid the night before. It's also a good rule of thumb to track your weight each day the week before your meet. This will help you stay on track and avoid any surprises when you step on the scale the day of the meet. Simply put, the last thing you'll want is to be over your weight class the day of the event. Keep me mind your home scale might not be 100% accurate so finding something comparable to the competition scale is best to ensure accuracy.

Once you've registered and weighed-in, you'll give the table your opening attempts. Some meet directors may ask for you to send your openers ahead of time via e-mail a week before the contest. Essentially, these are the weights that you will start out with for the competition itself. This will vary depending on how your training cycle went. To be cautious, it's safe to say that your maximum weight is something you can do for about three repetitions, even on a bad day. You should take a percentage from 87% to 92% of your one rep max. It usually needs to be in either five-pound increments or two and a half kilogram increments.

Let's take a lifter who has a max bench of 100 lbs. You obviously wouldn't be able to pick 87, for example since it is not in a 5lb increment. On a more conservative end, that lifter might open with 85 pounds on a moderate to middle-of-the-road approach. That lifter might open with 90 pounds if he or she wanted to be less conservative.

A not-so-conservative approach that I would not recommend for your first meet is opening with 95 pounds because that is over 93% of that lifter's max. You want to pick a weight that you can do for three reps in a very clean and good standard, even on an off day. Then if for some reason on the day of the meet you feel less than your best, you could also lower your opener before your plates start. They'll usually give you some sort of warning when you have to change your opener, which is typically about two minutes before you actually start. In stricter federation this is usually 5 minutes before the flight starts.

If your opener is slow and it's hard, it's difficult to come back from that from a mental standpoint because after that, it'll make you wonder, "what else can I do?" From a squat standpoint, it's the first step to the day and sets the tone of the meet. Many times, an athlete, especially for their first meet, can be very nervous going into their first squat. Even for me, after 12 years of experience, that opener squat will always be a little nerve-wracking. Once you get that opener squat out of the way though, your nerves will relax a bit. If you're going to a bit lighter on the opener, that's a great strategy that can set you up for a great day!

Your second attempt will build your momentum into the lift and will eliminate a lot of anxiousness. A good strategy is to try to do your best as possible. If you're going to go conservative on any one lift, especially for a raw meet it would probably be the squat or the bench.

The reason being for most raw lifters the deadlift is going to be the biggest part of their total (with some exceptions for people who excel in the squat) it'll be your strongest lift, which for most people is the deadlift. Aim for three-for-three in a squat especially for your first meet.

If you grind out a third attempt or get hurt, this will affect your bench and your deadlift. If your back is messed up in the first event, you'll be dead in the water afterwards and setting yourself up for failure. If you go three for three in a squat, you smash all your attempts, and you hit all your lifts, you'll be super confident going into the bench and your body will feel fresh going into the deadlift.

This three-for-three in the squat is a really good goal; it'll allow you to build more momentum going into the bench and ultimately the deadlift. This same strategy could work for the bench press, which is the weakest lift for most people, as it usually only accounts for about 20-25% of your actual total. As an example, of a 1,400 total, your squat will be 500, your deadlift will be 600, and your bench will only be 300.

Five pounds in the wrong direction on the bench

can really be a disaster, So again, I really try to advocate people to not do three too quickly since many times people make too big of a jump on the bench. You're using smaller muscle groups and won't be able to do as much. You're better off being a little more conservative on the bench, even if you're doing five or 10 pounds less since it won't make too much of a difference on your total.

It's usually a lot easier to make up five or 10 pounds on a deadlift, which is a bigger lift for most people than it is to make up five or 10 pounds on a bench. If you can, try five for six or six for six going into the deadlift. For those that are unfamiliar, you'll get three attempts in the squat three in the bench press, and three in the deadlift. You have nine lifts total for the day that are chanced to count.

Another reason why your openers should be light is that you are not allowed to go down, so you can only stick to the same weight or go up in weight. If you start opening too heavy, you could put yourself in a bad situation. If you miss all three lifts in any one discipline, that's a burn-out, and you'll be out of the meet, which is why it's very important you nail your first one.

If you want to be aggressive with any one event, I'd recommend doing so on your third deadlift since it's the last lift of the day. If for some reason something physically does go wrong, the meet is over at that point, so you can deal with it later. I'd recommend being a little more conservative on the squat and the bench, and again, if you want to do a huge push, do it during the final deadlift.

This strategy may be a little different for a raw with wraps or an equipped lifter since they'll probably need to rely on their squat a little bit more for bigger total but usually most people won't be wearing knee wraps for their first meet so this should not be a concern. That being said, I would still be conservative for the squat opener, and the same goes for the deadlift. It'll allow you get a total for the day. Really nailing those openers is important, as it sets the tone for the meet and helps build your momentum. So as you get more advanced if you are an accomplished squatter as you climb the ranks you might need to roll the dice more on your third squat attempt and be more aggressive to get a big total but this should not be the case for the beginner lifter.

As you get more competitive, you also might want to look at your deadlift attempts and compare them with the totals of other competitors. This could potentially influence your decisions and your seconds and thirds. For most contests, you could change your third deadlift multiple times to go for a win. This could be a good strategy to use as you improve and enter a national level or money meet.

You could also add up your squat and bench press going into the deadlift and see what your subtotal is. If you have a certain goal in mind, this could help you determine what you need to do to reach that goal.

For your first meet, I think it's really important to just try to hit a lot of the lifts. It's also great to build the experience because lifting on a platform will be way different than lifting in the gym. You'll have three judges that are judging you to a higher standard. Two out of three judges need to give you a white light for the lift account. If you're trying to be a little more conservative, do so for your first contest and try to go eight or nine for nine. Try and hit all your lifts. Also be sure to try and have fun. And hey, if you could hit some all-time PRs here and there—even better.

Any record is a personal record for your first time since it's the first time you ever set foot in the platform. You're establishing a total and trying to create a baseline. You're also trying to have a fun experience. Once you have that total, you can try and build on it every meet after that. You should just try and establish a baseline for yourself. That's the mindset and strategy going into your first contest.

After you give your openings to the table, you'll get your squat and/or bench height of the day. Make sure that you're wearing whatever shoes you'll be using for your squat and bench, and wear them at the correct height, which will be the height that you take the rack squats from. Be sure to give the head table your squat and bench heights, which will pretty much conclude the check-in process as far as the weigh-ins go.

A lot of federations have a 24-hour weight-in. I always recommend checking in and weighing in as early as possible. That way, it takes one thing out of the way. Other federations, like USAPL, require a two-hour weigh-in. Again, I'd highly recommend getting there as early as you can to avoid delay or hold-ups.

Chapter 5: Your Progression and Warm-Up Process

A COMMON MISTAKE I SEE in a lot of beginners is not writing down warm-ups. As an example, let's say your opening, just for the sake of ease and mathematic simplicity, you are opening at 100 pounds. Typically, since it's your first meet, you're probably a weak lifter. You'll want to give yourself at least 30 or 40 minutes of prep time. In a strict fed that runs fast you might have as little as twenty minutes to warm up in some cases. One thing that will really eat into your prep time is not being prepared with your warmups. If the empty bar is 45 pounds, you'll start at about five to seven warmup steps, completely depending on your starting skill level and strength.

If you're opening with 100 pounds, you might do the 45-pound bar for five reps. You might switch to 60 pounds after that for three reps. You might do 75 pounds for two, and then you'll switch to a single at 85, a single at 90, and then you'll hit your opener and go up on the platform. This would be just like a sample warm-up routine, but it's very important to actually write the whole process down. That way, it's one less thing you have to think about during the day of, since this day is typically extremely hectic.

Your coach will help you develop this warm-up strategy and will also encourage you to write them down for an easy reference. If you find yourself in a meet that may have a different bar than you're used to or if the weight is in a different measurement system, you can quickly and easily figure out how to translate and maneuver your warm-up process. A quick rule of thumb:

- A 45-pound bar is an empty bar
- 60 pounds is a 5 and a 2.5 on each side
- 75 pounds is a 10 and a 5 on each side
- 85 pounds is 2 10s on each side
- 90 pounds is 2 10s on each side and a 2.5 on each side

Obviously, I've been doing this awhile, so I've kind of got this memorized, but someone else may not have this committed to memory for their first meet. I'd actually write down what weights you want to put on the bar. I'm not that great with conversions into kilograms, so I rely on charts that are pretty easily accessible build the warm up plan based on the charts.

Loading chart for Eleiko plates (left half)

LBs	KGs	Plates + Collars			
133.2	60	1 x 15	1 x 2.5		
137.8	62.5	1 x 15	1 x 2.5	1 x 1.25	
143.2	65	1 x 20			
148.8	67.5	1 x 20	1 x 1.25		
154.3	70	1 x 20	1 x 2.5		
159.8	72.5	1 x 20	1 x 2.5	1 x 1.25	
165.3	75	1 x 25			
170.8	77.5	1 x 25	1 x 1.25		
176.3	80	1 x 25	1 x 2.5		
181.8	82.5	1 x 25	1 x 2.5	1 x 1.25	
187.4	85	1 x 25	1 x 5		
192.9	87.5	1 x 25	1 x 5	1 x 1.25	
198.4	90	1 x 25	1 x 5	1 x 2.5	
203.9	92.5	1 x 25	1 x 5	1 x 2.5	1 x 1.25
209.4	95	1 x 25	1 x 10		
214.9	97.5	1 x 25	1 x 10	1 x 1.25	
220.4	100	1 x 25	1 x 10	1 x 2.5	
225.9	102.5	1 x 25	1 x 10	1 x 2.5	1 x 1.25
231.4	105	1 x 25	1 x 15		
237	107.5	1 x 25	1 x 15	1 x 1.25	
242.5	110	1 x 25	1 x 15	1 x 2.5	
248	112.5	1 x 25	1 x 15	1 x 2.5	1 x 1.25
253.5	115	1 x 25			
259	117.5	1 x 25	1 x 20	1 x 1.25	
264.5	120	1 x 25	1 x 20	1 x 2.5	
270	122.5	1 x 25	1 x 20	1 x 2.5	1 x 1.25
275.5	125	2 x 25			
281	127.5	2 x 25	1 x 1.25		
286.6	130	2 x 25	1 x 2.5		
292.1	132.5	2 x 25	1 x 2.5	1 x 1.25	
297.6	135	2 x 25	1 x 5		
303.1	137.5	2 x 25	1 x 5	1 x 1.25	
308.6	140	2 x 25	1 x 5	1 x 2.5	

Loading chart for Eleiko plates (right half)

LBs	KGs	Plates + Collars			
314.1	142.5	2 X 25	1 X 5	1 x 2.5	1 x 1.25
319.6	145	2 x 25	1 x 10		
325.1	147.5	2 x 25	1 x 10	1 x 1.25	
330.7	150	2 x 25	1 x 10	1 x 2.5	
336.2	152.5	2 x 25	1 x 10	1 x 2.5	1 x 1.25
341.7	155	2 x 25	1 x 15		
347.2	157.5	2 x 25	1 x 15	1 x 1.25	
352.7	160	2 x 25	1 x 15	1 x 2.5	
358.2	162.5	2 x 25	1 X 15	1 x 2.5	1 X 1.25
363.7	165	2 x 25	1 x 20		
369.2	167.5	2 x 25	1 x 20	1 x 1.25	
374.8	170	2 x 25	1 x 20	1 x 2.5	
380.2	172.5	2 x 25	1 x 20	1 x 2.5	1 x 1.25
385.8	175	3 x 25			
391.3	177.5	3 x 25	1 x 1.25		
396.8	180	3 x 25	1 x 2.5		
402.3	182.5	3 x 25	1 x 2.5	1 x 1.25	
407.8	185	3 x 25	1 x 5		
413.3	187.5	3 x 25	1 x 5	1 x 1.25	
418.8	190	3 x 25	1 x 5	1 x 2.5	
424.3	192.5	3 x 25	1 x 5	1 x 2.5	1 x 1.25
429.9	195	3 x 25	1 x 10		
435.4	197.5	3 x 25	1 x 10	1 x 1.25	
440.9	200	3 x 25	1 x 10	1 x 2.5	
446.4	202.5	3 x 25	1 x 10	1 x 2.5	1 x 1.25
451.9	205	3 x 25	1 x 15		
457.4	207.5	3 x 25	1 x 15	1 x 1.25	
462.9	210	3 x 25	1 x 15	1 x 2.5	
468.4	212.5	3 x 25	1 x 15	1 x 2.5	1 x 1.25
473.9	215	3 x 25	1 x 20		
479.5	217.5	3 x 25	1 x 20	1 x 1.25	
485	220	3 x 25	1 x 20	1 x 2.5	
490.5	222.5	3 x 25	1 x 20	1 x 2.5	1 x 1.25

25 kg = red	15 kg = yellow	5 kg = white	1.25 kg = chrome
20 kg = blue	10 kg = green	2.5 kg = black	0.5 kg = chrome
			0.25 kg = chrome

KG conversation tables

I would also prep your food and water ahead of time. We're not endorsed by any of these products, but something like a Nuun tab is great: it provides electrolytes throughout the day. After you weigh in, you'll want to make sure that you continue to stay hydrated. Whether it's a 24-hour weigh-in or a two-hour weigh-in, it's great to hydrate with Nuun.

I also typically don't recommend a lot of sugar the day before the meet. Sugar the day of the meet if you are used to having that during training time can provide quick energy during the meet. I recommend eating foods you normally eat in smaller quantities through out the day without a lot of fat. Fat can slow down the digestion process.

If you're not cutting a lot of weight, which you actually shouldn't be, and if your weight is booked, it's great to stick to some kind of starchy carbohydrates like rice. You could add some things like soy sauce to add more sodium or more salt to your food to help keep you hydrated and keep your electrolytes high. The Nuun tablet can also help with that and is excellent for hydration and keeping your electrolytes down for the met. A good rule of thumb: keep your fats very low the day before the meet since fat takes longer to digest.

The day before a meet, it's best to avoid too much fat and calories or too much food in general. A good tactic I use is to cut off food around 7pm-8pm the night before a contest that starts at 8am-9am. This way, you'll have more than enough time to digest. If you have a lot of fats the night before, you'll impede the digestion and the flow of the nutrients the actually day of your competition, hindering your performance. Make sure that your nutrients are able to shuttle through your body and your muscles the day before, and make sure that the glycogen stores are very high so that the carbohydrates from the day before are helpful.

Some people consume some quick sugars the day of the meet, some even candy (but avoid the junk food you don't normally eat). If you want to have sugar, keep the fat low. Starchy carbohydrates mixed with some sugar (like diluted Pedialyte). Is also a great way to get that sugar without overdoing it.

You can absolutely drink water and should throughout the day—that's fine but make sure it's not so much it slow you down and you feel overly full. I would eat what you normally eat and I wouldn't consume anything you normally wouldn't. Be sure to get some sort of quick meal before each lift, and I would have small meals throughout the day so that it all just doesn't sit in your stomach. Keep the protein level low to moderate, and keep the fat super low or nonexistent. Have a little something before you squat, then have something immediately after you bench. Then following your deadlift, you can have whatever you want to celebrate and treat yourself. For most people they will focus on carbs and salt on game day.

When it comes to caffeine, especially if you're traditionally a caffeine junkie, a lot of people make the mistake of having too much caffeine too soon. I would actually recommend not having too much caffeine the week of the meet at all because you want to save that response for the actual meet to get a little boost. If you have one cup of coffee before you usually work out or if you have one scoop of pre-workout, trim it down to half of what you normally do and you can have some caffeine in smaller amounts before each event.

Nuun also makes an energy tab which has 40 mg of caffeine so you can dose appropriately. You can split tabs in half to get exactly the amount you need before each lift.

Too many people will have too much caffeine before they squat then end up crashing by the time they hit the deadlift. By regulating your intake and spreading out your doses by reduction, you can notice a drastic change. Having smaller doses of caffeine before each lift is a better strategy then having a lot of caffeine before your squat. If anything save a bigger dose of caffeine before the deadlift where you might need a boost to finish the day.

Just as important is of course getting plenty of sleep the night before. Try and relax. You can do some box breathing or a deep breathing exercise or any kind of meditation if you're into that. Basically, all you need to do is hold in your air for about three to five seconds, exhale for another three to five seconds, then hold it in for three to five seconds. This is a great way to clear your head and relax before your meet.

Yoga session

Many lifters like to listen to music to either calm their nerves or pump up their adrenaline. I recommend not going too crazy with the music too soon. I would start slowly dialing up the intensity as you're warming up. Be gradual with this intensity, as you don't want to kill your energy too soon or by the time you get to the deadlift. I try to stay out of the venue as long as possible to avoid over-stimulation. That being said every lifter is going to be different with how they "get in the zone" or "pysch up" so you need to find what works for you. But in general the best lifter seem to be able to remain calm until they get called and actually approach the bar. Save your energy for when you are actually lifting.

As mentioned before you warm ups are generally going to take about 30-40 minutes and you will start the flight before your flight goes. So if you are in Flight B start when A is lifting and if you are in Flight C start when B is lifting. If you are in Flight A you generally need to start warming up as soon as the rules briefing is over or sometimes even while it's going on depending on how the day is going to go. The meet director will generally have a time they aim to start flight A but it could also change so also double check with the meet director and people working the head table to ensure the pacing of your warm ups are appropriate and keeping you on track.

When it comes to your warm-ups, I recommend doing some sort of hip stretching movement before getting onto the barbell. Do whatever you normally do to prepare your body for the squat. It's a good rule of thumb to devote about 5-10 minutes of general stretching before doing the specific warm ups with the bar. After each event it's good to devote about five minutes of general stretching (if you normal prepare your workouts like this) to keep your body in motion and your blood flowing.

Mapping out your warm up will also depend on the flight you're in. Typically a flight is about 15 people, and in most situations, the less experience or lighter lifters will be in the earlier flights during the day. It's a good idea to warm up about 30 to 40 minutes before your flight starts. Pay attention to this upon your arrival so that your body is prepared and adjusted. Generally, the stronger you are, the more time you'll want to give yourself for the warm-up. Plus, it's overall better to be a bit earlier than have to rush your warm-ups.

Another great approach to your preparation is to

be very specific when it comes to your sets and what you plan on doing in each. Figure out when you'll add your belt or your wrist wraps. It's also a great idea to practice your commands while you're warming up—perfect the timing and the pacing so that your body develops the muscle memory before getting out onto the mat. Developing this even in the warm-up room is a great standard to set while competing. I also recommend saving some of your energy while warming up by asking a friend or your coach to spot you or load your plates. It'll save your back strength for the competition mat. The more you can focus on just lifting and not loading or thinking the better you are going to do!

For other miscellaneous things to bring, baby powder or chalk is a popular product for lifters to help with the deadlift—it just helps with the grip when your hands are sweating. Band-aids or a small first aid kit with athletic tape might also be helpful for any small cuts or breaks in skin. You'll develop callouses as you train, and those will rip and tear often, so having these things on hand will help. Extra socks and underwear are great backups so you can stay and feel fresh and dry during your competitions. A towel will also help you stay dry, so that's another great thing to be in the habit of bringing. It is better to have it and not need it then need it and not have it.

This should pretty much cover all of what's required prior to your first meet as well as the check-in process. Making a checklist is a great habit to get into in terms of what you need to bring, your warm-up ritual, and any kind of timeline that will keep you on track.

Chapter 6: Learning from Yourself and Some Rules

IT'S ALWAYS HELPFUL TO SEE yourself as others see you; by this, I mean you can record your lifts and be objective about them. Record your squats from the side so you can see your depth and bar path. I'd also video your bench presses from the side you can make sure that your butt is not coming off the bench. Videoing your deadlift from the side is also good so you can see your path and the angles will show you some of your major faults. It may not be the most aesthetic view, but it's a great view to actually analyze a technique.

One of the biggest faults is not achieving proper depth in the squat. For the bench press, the biggest one is probably coming off the bench, and the deadlift it's probably some sort of hitch, like supporting the body with the thighs or that kind of thing. Not locking up the critical joints in all the lift is a common fault: your hip and knee joints need to be fully extended at the lock-out. This is kind of rare in the squat, but if your knees aren't locked up fully or if your hips aren't locked up fully, and you're not standing erect, that'll result in a red light.

If your elbow isn't full locked out in the bench press, that's a red light. You need to obey all commands in all three lifts. If you jump a command from a judge in a squat, that'll be a no lift. If you jump a start command, the press command, or don't pause or balance your bench, that's a red light. If you drop the bar during a deadlift or if you start to put the bar back down or slam it down before the down command, that would be a no lift.

If there is any downward motion or any type of hiccup in any three lifts, that can be a no lift. It cannot travel downward once you start the ascent, coming out of the hold of the squat, coming off your chest at the bench press, or lifting the bar up from the floor. If there is any downward motion once the bar comes back down, even if it's slight, that'll result in a no lift.

Faults can happen in any of the three lifts. If you stumble during the lift, this can happen. If your foot slips during the bench press, or if you stumble coming out of a deadlift or fall backwards to take a step with the weight, that's also a no lift.

In some federations, like the USAPL, the start command is going to be a bit longer because the two side judges need to approve that the athlete is ready to start before the head judge actually gives you a signal. In the USAPL, you need to have your feet flattened on the ground, and you need to have the head in contact with the bench. These are all things that can be cause for disqualification.

Conclusion

IT'S SO IMPORTANT TO REMEMBER why you started. It's important to remember that no one is getting paid millions to be a powerlifter at this point. Go out there and have fun, have a good time. Of course, you could take it seriously. Of course, you'll want to work really hard, but just don't forget to have fun. It really does sound cliché, but what's awesome about powerlifting is that you can do it at any age, you could start at any age, and you can do this for the whole life you wanted.

Make sure you enjoy the process. Don't get frustrated if you don't do as well as you wanted. Try and celebrate the small wins and build on them. The other thing I would just say is that after the meet is over, there is so much that goes into the contest – make sure you shake the judges' hands, whether you win, lose, or draw. This shows good sportsmanship, and it's a reminder that ultimately, everyone is there to be civil. All these things are what make powerlifting so great. If you get a coach, make sure you thank them.

Parting Words

One thing that I used to say is, "Work hard, be consistent, and don't give up. Have fun, and keep pushing.

PS Here is a Link to our YT Channel Video that gives a 10 minute overview of Powerlifting Rules

https://www.youtube.com/watch?v=f4TjlwDTZjc&t=16s

About The Author

John Gaglione is a strength coach based out of Long Island, New York. John trains people from all walks of life at his facility, which is located in Farmingdale, New York. He specializes in improving maximal strength for both athletes and "average Joes" alike. He currently leads a powerlifting team of over 40 members. At the time of this writing he has helped over 50 lifters achieve national ranking in their division.

John has written many strength and conditioning articles for major online publications, such as Men's Health, Elite Fitness Systems, Testosterone Nation, and One Result. He is the featured strength & conditioning author for the book Long Island Wrestling Association. John has been a featured speaker at several schools, including Cortland and Hofstra Universities – for their exercise science programs.

As an avid strength athlete, John also has a lot of "under the bar experience," and he has competed in the sport of powerlifting for over a decade. He has the best competition lifts: an 900 Squat, 575 Bench, and a 640 Deadlift.

If you would like to learn more about John, you can reach him at *john@gaglionestrength.com*.

About The Author

Train with Gaglione Strength

For locals, you can request a complimentary session and consultation by sending an e-mail to john@gaglionestrength.com with the subject line "Are You Ready To Compete" and we will get your scheduled for your session.

For those who are not in the Tri-state area, you can take full advantage of our Elite Distance Coaching program by going to sending an e-mail to john@gaglionestrength.com with the subject line "Online Coaching Are You Ready To Compete" for a special discounted rate exclusive only to our readers.

If are a beginner or a seasoned veteran in the sport, we can help you! Our most accomplished lifter Mark Greenstein, who, at the time of this book, is ranked 5th best all time in the world in the sport of powerlifting in the 198 class with an 1825 total.

No matter where you are or what level you are at we can help you get to the next one and help you become the strongest version of you!

ARE YOU READY TO COMPETE?

Whether you are just starting our or you are already elite we can help you! Don't be shy and contact us today with any questions you may have! We wish you luck on your journey to become a stronger you!

Made in USA - North Chelmsford, MA
1177389_9781073036813
10.08.2020 1617